YOUR KNOWLEDGE HAS VALUE

AF143494

- We will publish your bachelor's and master's thesis, essays and papers

- Your own eBook and book - sold worldwide in all relevant shops

- Earn money with each sale

Upload your text at www.GRIN.com and publish for free

Alfons Unmüßig

Software Defect Prevention for better Software Quality

Key Determinants and their interlinked effects

GRIN Publishing

Bibliographic information published by the German National Library:

The German National Library lists this publication in the National Bibliography; detailed bibliographic data are available on the Internet at http://dnb.dnb.de .

This book is copyright material and must not be copied, reproduced, transferred, distributed, leased, licensed or publicly performed or used in any way except as specifically permitted in writing by the publishers, as allowed under the terms and conditions under which it was purchased or as strictly permitted by applicable copyright law. Any unauthorized distribution or use of this text may be a direct infringement of the author s and publisher s rights and those responsible may be liable in law accordingly.

Imprint:

Copyright © 2012 GRIN Verlag GmbH
Print and binding: Books on Demand GmbH, Norderstedt Germany
ISBN: 978-3-656-20659-0

This book at GRIN:

http://www.grin.com/en/e-book/195119/software-defect-prevention-for-better-software-quality

GRIN - Your knowledge has value

Since its foundation in 1998, GRIN has specialized in publishing academic texts by students, college teachers and other academics as e-book and printed book. The website www.grin.com is an ideal platform for presenting term papers, final papers, scientific essays, dissertations and specialist books.

Visit us on the internet:

http://www.grin.com/

http://www.facebook.com/grincom

http://www.twitter.com/grin_com

Systemic Software-Defect-Prevention for better Software Quality

- Key Determinants and their interlinked effects -

Content

Systemic Software-Defect-Prevention for better Software-Quality

- Key Determinants and their interlinked effects -

Abstract

This work aims to propose a qualitative "starter model" for a new software defect prevention for better Software Quality. Software defect prevention methods and models have made substantial progress in recent years. But this still falls short of the needs of today and the future. One contribution is a qualitative model that takes into account key determinants and their interlinked effects. The model is based on System Dynamics and the elements involved in the software development process, e.g. the human being, management, members of staff, work psychology, quality, methods, organizations, customer, culture etc. Current research status comprises 15 identified important key determinants, their respective strength, interrelationships and dynamics. The model is operationalized with a software tool capable of modelling all the key determinants defined, their effect directions and other data of the comprehensive matrix they make up. With the research results made, the new defect prevention model shows promise. The research is due to continue further in order to contribute to improved defect prevention in the software development process. The number of key determinants, their respective strength etc. be will be 140 in the final research work.

Keywords: Systemic, software, software development, Software-quality, defects, defect prevention, Determinants, System Dynamics, qualitative model, the human being, process, methods, technology, organization.

1. Starting Position and Problem Definition

Over the past years, software complexity has been rising steadily, with more complex processes in all areas of life progressively automated through software. Spectacular software defects over the last years have put man and nature at risk, causing extensive cost and frustrating customers. Consequently, software defect prevention in the software development process is growing in importance. Today's defect prevention techniques have made substantial progress over the last years in a contribution to better defect prevention. This paper aims via comprehensive systemic approach that takes account of key determinants and their interlinked effects to further improvements to software defect prevention. The model is not meant to replace current defect prevention procedures but rather to consequently expand and complement the procedures.

The key focus in the research effort is on the first three phases (Requirement Analysis, Specification and Design) of the software development process. Based on the results of the research of available sources and in author's own experience, 50 to 70 % of all defects come about in these three first development phases, with most only found in later phases.

2. Desk Research and Theoretical Background

2.1 Software Development Process
Methods

Different methods find use in the software development process. Consequently, the process may be implemented with various tools and methods. The methods and CASE (= Computer Aided Software Engineering) tools employed are major determinants of productivity and defect prevention efficiency (Balzert 1998, p. 15).

Process-/Procedure Models

For the development of software, process and procedure models are in use. A process model structures the software development process into activities and results (see Fig. 1). The model defines rules governing the scope of the activities, their course and output. The activities and results fall under different types of operations such as project management. Process models further also define the relevant roles, tools and methods.

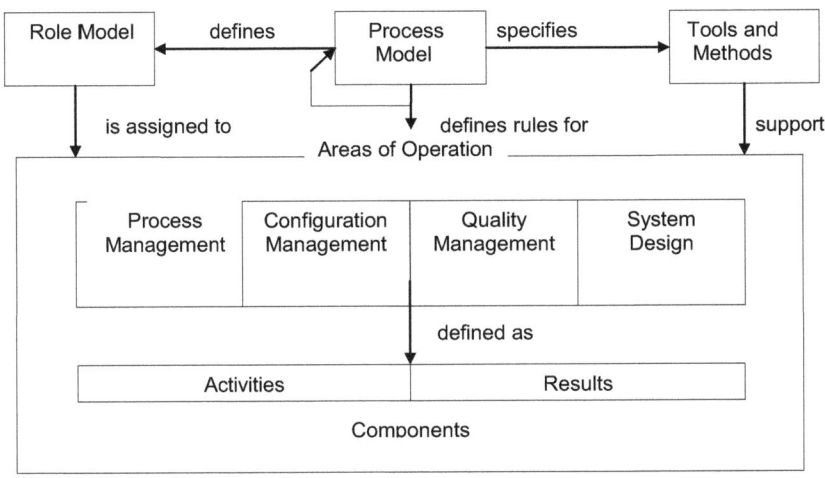

FIG. 1: PROCESS MODEL

(Source: Bunse 2008, p. 4)

2.2 Software Defects

Software defects mainly are a result of human error in the development process. As the development process entails several phases, the defects may result e.g. from: Misconceptions in initial requirements; Design inadequacies; Programming errors. Defects not detected in the respective development phases stages may add and multiply in follow-up development phases by causing further defects. Hence a defect summation effect applies (Wallmüller 2001, p. 15).

3. Software Defect Prevention

Defect prevention is a key activity in the software development process. Late defect detection adds massively to costs. According to various analyses and author's own experience, defect elimination costs as a variable multiply by a factor of about five to ten for each phase in the sequence. Consequently, defect prevention should be pursued as the primary aim. The following **analytical, constructive, organizational** and **psychological** defect prevention actions and **Software Process Improvement Models** are important Inputs for the present Systemic Defect Prevention Model. They are part of a number of different sources of applicable determinants.

3.1 Outline of the four classes of defect prevention actions:

a. Analytical Quality Actions

Analytical quality actions are implemented e.g. in order to verify current quality levels. The examinations do not establish absolute certainty as regards conformity/non-conformity of a product.

b. Constructive Quality Actions

Constructive quality actions mainly aim at defect prevention e.g. use of Process Models and Methods.

c. Organizational Quality Actions

Organizational actions include the design, implementation and maintenance of e.g. a corporate Quality Management System, Project Management System and others.

d. Psychological Prevention Actions/People Actions

Software development should not be considered a purely technical procedure only. As software development is carried by the human input (the development team), communication processes, leadership, quality culture and other variables this entails are key to the output quality.

3.2 Software Process Improvement Models for Defect Prevention

Process improvements may be implemented in a number of different ways such as under the classical PDCA (**P**lan, **D**o, **C**heck, **A**ct) cycle or by way of capability maturity models. An advantage to using capability maturity models, they systematically impose successful practices on different models. Examples of capability maturity models include CMMI or SPICE (Hörmann, 2006, p. 5).

3.3 Costs and Benefits of Practical Software Defect Prevention

Fig. 2 shows that most defects are produced in the first two phases of Requirements and Design but are only recognized in later phases. For instance in the Requirements phase, 10% defects are produced but only 3 % detected by Requirement Review. Such circumstances always have a negative effect on costs.

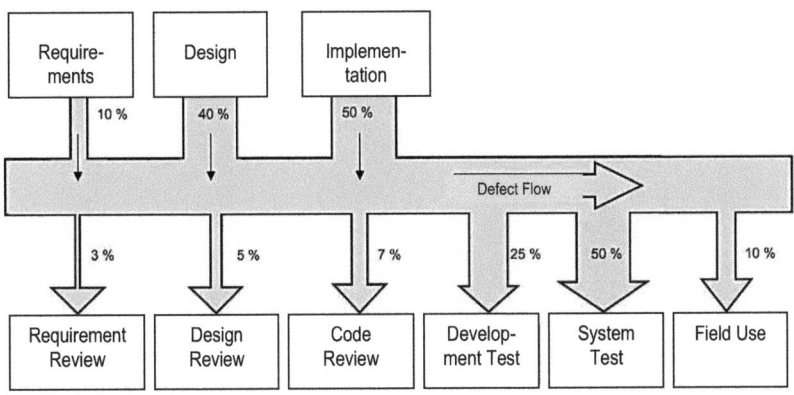

FIG. 2: PHASES OF OCCURENCE AND ELIMINATION OF SOFTWARE DEFECTS
(Source: Masing 2007, p. 835)

3.4 Summary of Desk Research and Theoretical Background

Software Development Process

In software development processes, progress has been made in recent years. This has been facilitated e.g. through the use of process models, optimization in processes, new and improved methods, professional project and risk management, new and improved tools and other systematic means. Further improvements are needed e.g. in requirement analysis.

Defect Prevention in the Software Development Process

Defect prevention also saw improvements in recent years credit to optimization in software development processes. The newly implemented processes in defect prevention such as design-related quality actions, quality methods and particularly the use of capability maturity models all add to the difference. Nevertheless, the number of defects still remains high. Further research is needed into software development and defect prevention.

This paper aims by means of a comprehensive and interlinked perspective that includes the human factor to help optimize defect prevention specifically in the phases of Requirement Analysis, Specification and Design.

4. Method

The research is performed using a theoretical and an empirical concept respectively.

4.1 Concept Design

Based on the insights gained with scientific methods in the research of available sources, a concept design is compiled for systemic defect prevention. Related themes and topics such as organization, leadership and quality culture also are included in the examination. The systemic concept is very closely related to complex network systems.

The assumptions drawn based on the research of available sources and author's personal experience will be complemented by an empirical survey. The persons interviewed include managerial functions and experts in the areas of Software development and Software Quality Management. The expert interviews are not a part of this paper, as they will be done in a later research phase.

Finding the Method for Solving Problems in Complex Network Systems

Method

For the present model of "Systemic Defect Prevention", a method is required to deal with complex network systems. The methods for dealing with complexity are subject to 26 criteria according to Grossmann (Grossmann 1992, p. 44). Some of the criteria are: providing for a large number of components; reflecting mutual relationships between the components; providing for changing cause and effect chains. Further needed is emphasis on facts, clarity, dynamics, creativity, inclusion of social aspects and human interactions, openness and promotion of integration.

In order to be able to effectively deal with complexity and hence facilitate systemic defect prevention, a model has to include both the factual and behaviour - related dimensions. In Grossmann (1992, p. 188), nine concepts are investigated. A conclusion based on comprehensive analysis of the nine concepts left two remaining: Thinking in Networks and the Sensitivity Model (SM). The final decision was – after a consideration of various aspects – for "Thinking in Networks".

For operationalzing the "Sensitivity Model" and "Thinking in Networks" methods/models, software tools have been developed by universities and the industry. For purposes herein, the "Consideo Modeler" modeling tool by Consideo GmbH in Lübeck, Germany has been chosen that is based on the "Thinking in Networks" model.

4.2 Systemic Thinking /Cross-linked Thinking

Systemic thinking amounts to identifying mutual interdependencies and the rules behind causal interactions (Hamilton 2007, p. 110). Fig. 3 shows an example systemic software development process. Hints and ideas for solving the problem of "comprehensive interlinked defect prevention in the software development process" have been supplied among others by the following authors who spearheaded research into systemic thinking:

(Dörner, 2008); (Gomez/Probst, 1987); (Gomez/Probst, 1997); (Senge, 1996); (Veester, 2007).

Systemic thinking relies on six steps:

(1) *Defining objectives and modelling the problem situation*

(2) *Analyzing causal chains*

(3) *Exploring and interpreting possible trends in the future*

(4) *Exploring control options*

(5) *Planning strategies and actions*

(6) *Implementing the problem solution*

Systemic Software Development

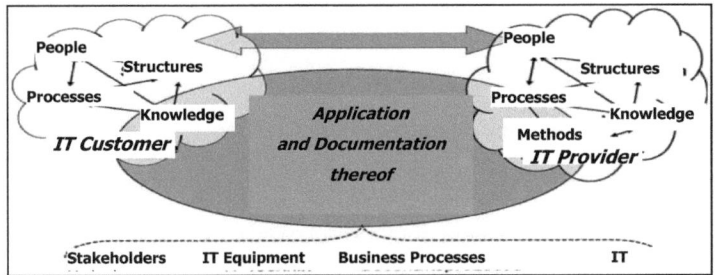

Classical Software Development

FIG. 3: SYSTEMIC SOFTWARE DEVELOPMENT

(Source: Hamilton 2008, p. 91)

5. The Model Concept

5.1 Model Structure

Applicable determinants are identified based on the insights of a number of disciplines. The key focus areas are:

- Processes, activities, methods and models from software development and quality management
- The human factor
- Other disciplines dealing with defect prevention such as medicine, aviation, work psychology etc.

The model amounts to a generic model that in its practical application splits further into sublevels if e.g. more as 15 Determinants. In this paper, no such "sublevel" is presented.

The determinants at work, their interlinked effects, effect directions and effect intensities are modelled with the "Consideo Modeler" tool.

Objective of the model

- The model is meant to represent in a true-to-reality manner the complex applicable interdependencies and causal chains
- The use of insights from other sources and disciplines such as medicine, psychology and culture shall provide new incentives to further improve software defect prevention.

System Theory based Assessment

In order to develop a network matrix model for analyzing the problem and finding solutions, insight is needed into causal relationships between the variables involved (Gomez/Probst 1997, p. 72).

Interdependencies are quantifiable through the following three aspects:

1. In their effect: - Is there a promotive or inhibitive/stabilizing effect?
2. According to intensity: - Is it weak, moderate or strong?
3. According to temporal presence: - Is the causal effect short, medium or long in duration?

5.2 Identifying the Determinants

For identifying relevant determinants, the following "sources" are used: techniques, models and activities used in software development and in quality processes, case study, human factor-related aspects and insights from other disciplines. For further details, refer to "Software Defect Prevention" herein and relevant sources, such as Masing (2007), Balzert (1998), Gerlich (2005), Hoffmann (2008), Wallmüller (2001, 2011).

5.3 Examination of Applicable Determinants Based on

- **Case Study**

In order to determine applicable determinants for purposes of comprehensive defect prevention based on real customer projects, the author and his team carried out an RCA in the firm with follow-up evaluation of results.

The results of the case study largely confirm the desk research findings and provide additional new insights of use in future defect prevention.

A higher number of reviews of specifications and design documents greatly improves defect prevention and hence also helps reduce defect costs.

- With software developers, testers and quality experts working closely in conjunction, team spirit is promoted and a boost to quality culture is achieved that benefits defect prevention.

- **Determinants that Relate to the Human Factor**

At present, software still is prevalently compiled by humans. This means the key defect source for software errors is the human factor. Generally at the individual human level, the cause and effect logic does not always apply. The human performance potential is shaped by a comprehensive variety of factors. Figure 4 provides a visual analogy to the causal origin of human defects in the form of the Swiss Cheese Model based on J.T. Reason (1990/2008).

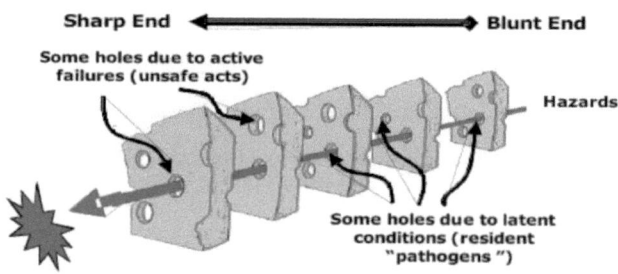

FIG. 4: SWISS CHEESE MODEL: THE CAUSALITY OF HUMAN ERROR (Source: in reference to J.T. Reason)

J.T.Reason essentially differentiates between **latent and active** defects. **Latent** defects relate causally e.g. to the organization where some activities are not defined in operating instructions for the respective task/workplace. **Active** defects refer to human error while performing the actual task.

- **Determinants from other Disciplines**

The following variables have been derived from other disciplines e.g. such as work psychology, organization theory and culture: workload and stress at work, emergent software defects, corporate culture and quality culture.

5.4 Comments on Target Variable and Determinants

• *Target Variable*

The target variable is identifiable with the factor of **"1 successful failure prevention"** in the center of Figure 5.

• *Determinants*

The following determinants affect the target variable directly or indirectly.

- *20 Clearly defined customer requirements*

The core element in defect prevention is a precise definition of requirements.

- *3 Employee workload and stress*

The above and further determinants that relate to this area have a negative effect in defect prevention by causing e.g. lower employee concentration.

- *4 Attained level of process maturity*

Capability maturity models such as SPICE and CMMI amount to dedicated tools for process improvement purposes, hence also determinants in defect prevention. Process maturity levels are measured in grades where for instance in CMMI, the top grade is Level 5.

- *5 Emergent software defects*

Emergence refers in philosophy and psychology to a phenomenon where specific properties or behavior of a whole cannot be derived from the sum of behavior of its individual parts (Hamilton 2007, p. 119). Applied to software, emergent defects may come about through instable hardware.

- *6 Staff expertise and empirical experience*

Professional expertise and empirical experience of individuals are essential to defect prevention.

- *7 Application software complexity*

  Complexity of target application software also is a key determinant as it may drive complex and to some part, in conjunction with instable hardware, even emergent defects.

- *8 Leadership qualities in management*

  Leadership is defined in expert sources in a number of different ways, some of which are: Being a role model (Seghezzi 2007, p. 79) and actively dealing with topics (in reference to Strunz 2001, p. 168); Directing staff towards a vision so that they respond in a motivated manner; Making staff understand the context by means of suitable communication (employee orientation).

- *9 A learning organization*

  Continuous learning in organization is a factor of essential importance in complex systems. Available sources such as Senge (2008) provide comprehensive examinations of the topic.

- *10 Motivated employees*

  Motivation is interpreted as the cause for a specific human behavior (Strunz 2001, p. 49). As a result, the employee becomes directed towards a specific objective. Applied to the effort herein, the objective is "to avoid software defects". Available sources deal comprehensively with the topic which is why it shall not be discussed in more detail herein.

- *11 Open and fair communication & feedback*

  Within the comprehensive variety of communication, open communication that includes feedback promotes fairness, the will to listen and the readiness to report defects including software defects without fear. Open communication also promotes motivation.

- *12 Requirement analysis quality*

  The quality of the requirement analysis and understanding customer needs and expectations is a difficult and complex task as the process frequently involves two individuals or cultures that think in different patterns. The customer defines and/or proclaims their expectations in a particular 'language' which differs from that of the supplier and/or software developer. A 'language' signifies in this context also a different culture.

- *13 Quality culture*

For successful defect prevention, the quality culture practiced by the firm is key as the quality culture that grows out of corporate culture is an integral part of enterprise quality (Seghezzi 1996, p. 181). Managerial functions should be a role model in quality matters in their everyday stances and attitudes.

- *14 Unstable hardware*

Unstable hardware frequently drives emergent software defects that are difficult to identify. The process of defect location entails a complex effort that often branches into wrong directions with frustration as a result.

- *15 Corporate culture*

Corporate culture is the entirety of shared values, standards, stances and attitudes that shape the decisions, actions and behavior of the members of the organization (Gabler, a). Consequently, the attitudes towards successful defect prevention essentially grow out of corporate culture. For further discourse, refer to Schein (2003).

5.5 Causal interdependencies, their effect directions and effect intensities

In the following parts, some causal interdependencies, their effect directions, effect intensities and temporal variations are briefly outlined. In the network matrix visualization in Fig. 5, the effect direction always is indicated by an arrow and the effect intensity by the line width and/or the attached numerical indication, where 10=weak, 17=moderate, 25=strong. Strikethrough arrows indicate a temporal delay. One strikethrough in a line that connects the determinants amounts to one temporal unit. The temporal unit (second, minute,...) is definable in Modeller. In this particular model, a temporal unit is approximately equal to one year.

- *2 Clearly specified customer expectations → 1 successful failure prevention*
  Clear and precise specifications of customer expectations are the initial reference basis in defect prevention, hence have a direct effect. They strongly affect defect prevention as wrong or missing specifications may have fatal consequences.

- *2 Clearly specified customer expectations → 12 Application software complexity*
  Clear and precise specifications moderately lower the complexity of application software.

- *2 Clearly specified customer expectations → 12 Requirement analysis quality*
  The quality of customer expectations has a moderate positive effect on requirement analysis quality.

- *3 Employee Workload and stress → 10 Motivated employees*
  Higher workload and stress intensity has a moderate negative effect on employee motivation.

- *5 Emergent software defects → 1 successful failure prevention*
  Due to non-controllability of emergent software defects, they have a moderate negative effect on successful defect prevention.

- *5 Emergent software defects → 10 Motivated employees*
  Emergent software defects also have a fair negative effect on employee motivation.

Further interdependencies and their respective effect directions and intensities are provided in the network matrix visualization in Figure 5 and the weighting matrix in Figure 6.

6. Results

Visualization, Mutual Effects and Effect Intensities of Determinants

By means of Consideo Modeler, the determinants are comprised into a generic model with a network matrix structure and analyzed.

6.1 Visualizations and Analyses

The following Fig. 5 shows the interdependencies, effect directions and effect intensities of applicable determinants. The target variable of "successful defect prevention" is shown in the middle. For each determinant, its interdependencies (arrows), effect intensities (numerical indications) and a plus or minus sign are indicated. A plus sign before the numerical intensity signifies in addition to the effect direction its promotive effect, a minus sign its inhibitive effect.

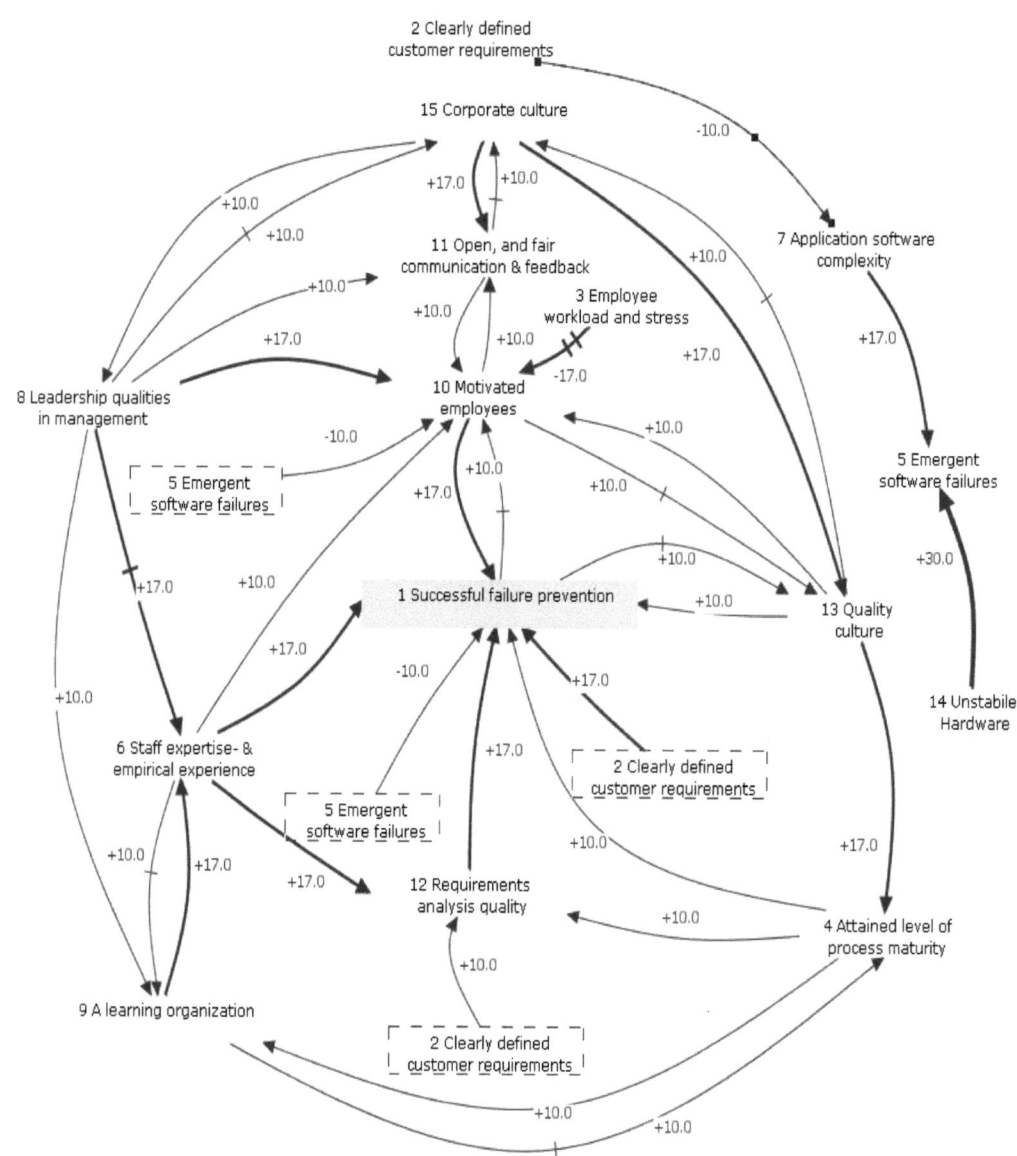

FIG. 5: THE DETERMINANTS IN A NETWORK OF INTERDEPENDENCIES

(Author's own visualization using Consideo Modeler)

The following Fig. 6 shows the weighting matrix that provides percentage indications of the effects of the different determinants within the network (effect direction FROM/TO on the y- and x-axes respectively).

The visualization informs of the weighting of the different factors. For instance a learning organization (y-axis, row 10) participates with 17 % in the effect on professional expertise and empirical experience (x-axis, column 7). The sum of values in each column of the weighting matrix must not exceed 100%. A sum lower than 100% indicates that there are additional determinants to those included in the systemic visualization.

Software-Defectprevention Comenius University Bratislava SK for_Singapore_2011

		1	2	3	4	5	6	7	8	9	10	11	12	13	14	15
1	1 Successful failure pr...					10	10									
2	2 Clearly defined cust...	17										10			10	
3	11 Open, and fair com...				10		10									
4	15 Corporate culture			17		17			10							
5	13 Quality culture	10			10		10									17
6	10 Motivated employees	17		10		10										
7	6 Staff expertise- & e...	17					10				10				17	
8	8 Leadership qualities ...			10	10		17	17			10					
9	3 Employee workload ...						17									
10	9 A learning organizati...							17								10
11	7 Application software ...													17		
12	14 Unstabile Hardware													30		
13	5 Emergent software f...	10					10									
14	12 Requirements analy...	17														
15	4 Attained level of pro...	10									10				10	
	Summe	98	0	37	30	37	84	34	10	0	30	10	0	47	37	27

FIG. 6: WEIGHTING MATRIX

(Author's own visualization using Consideo Modeler)

6.2 Explanation of Elements in the Result Matrix

Based on the cause and effect relationships held including the respective effect directions, intensities and temporal delays (and the resulting self-amplified and balancing feedback loops), the result matrix in Fig. 7 provides all the determinants that directly or indirectly affect the chosen factor, which in this case is the **target variable of "successful defect prevention"**. On the x-axis, the total effect intensity (sum of direct and indirect effect intensities of each determinant relative to chosen factor (positive or negative). The y-axis shows changes in the effect intensity of the determinants on a timeline (increase or decrease). This gives rise to four different quadrants shown in Fig. 7 (the result matrix):

1. *The upper right area* (progressively promotive): determinants that in the short term have positive effect, with an outlook of even more pronounced positive impact in the mid to long term. The weight of the determinants grows over periods of time as they are largely involved in self-amplified feedback loops and/or trigger the loops. The determinants are the most effective levers for positive development in chosen factor.

2. *The lower right area* (degressively promotive): determinants that in the short term have positive effect, with mid- to long-term outlook of less strong positive impact. The weight of the determinants declines over periods of time as they are largely involved in balancing feedback loops and/or trigger the loops.

3. *The lower left area* (progressively inhibitive): determinants that in the short term have negative effect, with an outlook of even more significant negative impact in the mid to long term. The weight of the determinants grows over periods of time as they are largely involved in self-amplified feedback loops and/or trigger the loops. The determinants are the most effective levers for negative development in chosen factor.

4. *The upper left area* (degressively inhibitive): determinants that in the short term have negative effect, with an outlook of less pronounced negative impact in the mid to long term. The weight of the determinants declines over periods of time as they are largely involved in balancing feedback loops and/or trigger the loops.

5. The numerical codes and names of the determinants are provided on the right in the matrix.

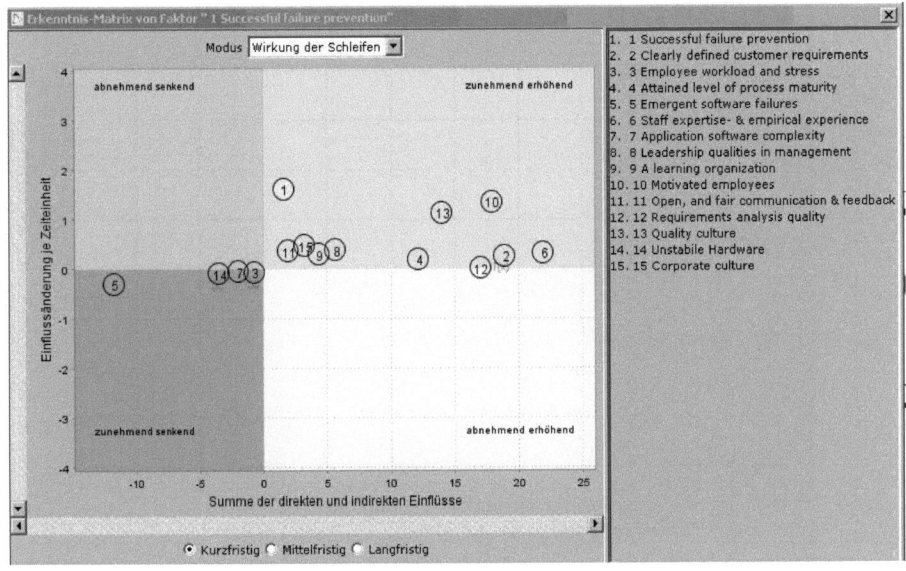

FIG. 7: RESULT MATRIX, short-term perspective

(Author's own visualization using Consideo Modeler)

6.3 Analysis of determinants in the result matrix

The analysis of the result matrix provides the gist of output of present effort. The matrix entails a comparison of the effects of the determinants on a freely choosable factor which in this particular case is the **target variable of "successful defect prevention"** assigned **number 1**. For each determinant included, its effect intensity is shown via the x- and y-axes relative to chosen factor (here: the target variable) The result matrix in Fig. 7 shows the short-term effects and Fig. 8 the long-term effects respectively of the determinants on successful defect prevention.

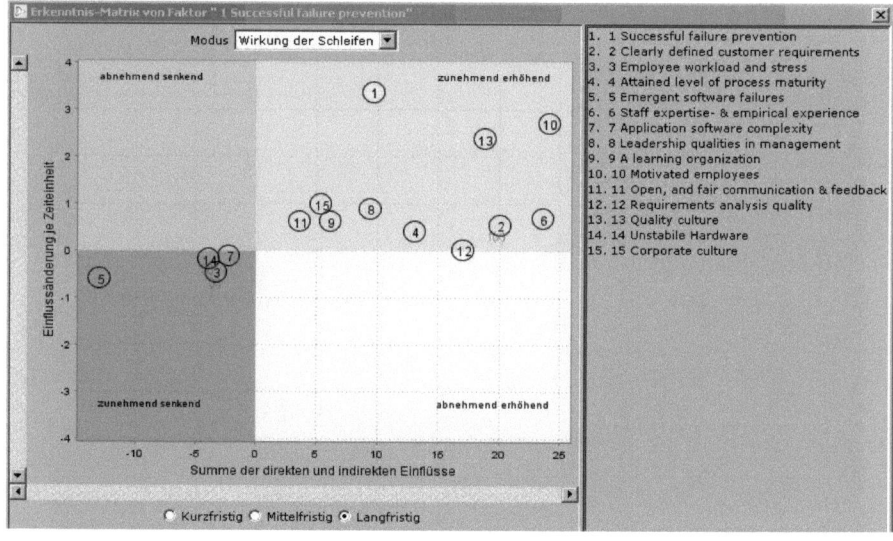

FIG. 8: RESULT MATRIX, long-term perspective

(Author's own visualization using Consideo Modeler)

7. Discussion and Conclusion

7.1 Discussion

In this part, the **short-term effects** held in **Figure 7** and **long-term** effects held in **Figure 8** are discussed of applicable determinants including respective impacts and possible actions.

The determinants No. 10 (Motivated Employees) and No. 13 (Quality Culture) in the upper right quadrant in Fig. 7 have a strongly positive effect in the short term (on an ad hoc basis) which even grows further in intensity over long term as seen in Fig. 8. The weight of the determinants grows, hence they are identifiable as key levers in comprehensive defect prevention. This is evident also from the new position of the target variable identified as No. 1 in the upper right quadrant in the visualization.

The determinants No. 2 (Clearly Specified Customer Expectations), No. 4 (Level of Process Maturity) and No. 6 (Staff expertise and empirical experience) in Fig. 7 have a strong effect in the short term (as they score high on the x-axis) but a relatively moderate positive effect in future projection (as they show no increase on the y-axis, see Fig. 8). The remaining determinants Nos. 8 (Leadership qualities in management), 9 (A learning organization), 11(Open, and fair communication) and 15 (Corporate culture) in the quadrant, though having a positive effect, show minimum increase in the effect intensity in the future. This is evident from Figures 7 and 8. The determinant No. 12 (Requirements analysis quality) in Figures 7 and 8 has a constant effect intensity both in the short and long term at identical x-axis values. Consequently, the variable exhibits no dynamics.

The determinants No. 3 (Employee workload and stress), No. 7 (Application software complexity) and No. 14 (Unstable Hardware) in the lower left quadrant in Fig. 7 already have a negative short-term effect on the target variable. Fig. 8 implies further moderate negative developments in the long term in both the x- and y-axis values in relation to the target variable. The determinant No. 5 (Emergent Software Defects) has a fairly strong negative effect in the short term given its distinct x-axis value that further grows in the long term with an even more pronounced y-axis value.

7.2 Conclusion

The model output and discussion comprise based on a quality-oriented approach the short- and long-term status and trends in applicable interdependencies and the significance of individual determinants. The results provide indications as to where actions/system interventions are needed. The most significant determinants with positive effect in defect prevention numbered 2 (Clearly defined customer requirements), 6 (Staff expertise-& empirical experience), 10 (Motivated employees) and 13 (Quality culture) need reinforcement.

The determinants numbered 8 (Leadership qualities), 9 (A learning organization), 11 (Open, and fair communication & feedback), 12 (Requirements analysis quality) and 15 (Corporate culture) positioned in the upper right quadrant of "progressively promotive" have a moderate effect intensity, hence necessitate reinforcement through adequate measures.

The determinants numbered 3 (Employee workload and stress), 5 (Emergent software defects), 7 (Application software complexity) and 14 (Unstable hardware) have an effect direction that runs contrary to defect prevention, hence need optimization through targeted system interventions. The actual causes are identifiable with emergent software defects, workload and stress at work and application software complexity. The causal background needs to be analyzed of the 3 determinants with negative effect and the causes avoided in the future.

The model further can be optimized in two additional ways.

1. Expand the model with further determinants with subsequent new verification and optimization.

   (this model expansion by the author currently is under development)

2. Develop and analyze a highly comprehensive quantitative model

Generally, a note is due that any actions and model expansions made need to be verified for their interlinked effects and balanced accordingly as the determinants function in a matrix of mutual relationships and consequently also need assessment in a relationship matrix.

As further research task, the model expansion may be recommended to cover the entire software lifecycle.

References

Balzert, H.F. (1998). **Lehrbuch der Software-Technik**; Software-Management, Software-Qualitätssicherung, Unternehmensmodellierung. Spektrum, Akademischer Verlag Heidelberg/Berlin

Bunse, C./Knethen, A. (2008). **Vorgehensmodelle Kompakt**; Spektrum Akademischer Verlag Heidelberg

Dörner, D. (2008). **Die Logik des Misslingens**; Strategisches Denken in komplexen Situationen; Powohlt Taschenbuch Verlag 7. Auflage

Gerlich, Ra. & Re. (2005). **111 Thesen zur erfolgreichen Softwareentwicklung**; Springer Verlag, Berlin/Heidelberg

Gomez, P., Probst, G. (1987). **Vernetztes Denken im Management**; Die Orientierung Nr. 89, CH-Bern, Schweizerische Volksbank

Gomez, P., Probst, G. (1997). **Die Praxis des ganzheitlichen Problemlösens**; Vernetzt denken, Unternehmerisch handeln, Persönlich überzeugen; 2. überarbeitete Auflage; Bern, Stuttgart, Wien,

Grossmann, C. (1992). **Komplexitätsbewältigung im Management**; Anleitungen, integrierte Methodik und Anwendungsbeispiele; Verlag GCN, Winterthur

Hamilton, P. (2007). Dynaxity; **Management von Dynamik und Komplexität im Softwarebau;** Springer Verlag Berlin Heidelberg

Hamilton, P. (2008). **Wege aus der Softwarekrise**; Springer Verlag Berlin Heidelberg

Hörmann, K./Dittmann, L./Hindel, B. (2006). **SPICE in der Praxis**; Interpretationshilfe für Anwender und Assessoren, basierend auf ISO/IEC 15504, dpunkt.Verlag, Heidelberg

Hoffman, D. W. (2008). **Software Qualität**; Springer-Verlag, Berlin Heidelberg

Masing, W. (2007). **Handbuch Qualitätsmanagement**; Herausgegeben von T. Pfeifer/R. Schmitt, 5., vollständig neu bearbeitete Auflage, Hanser Verlag München

Reason, I. (1990/2008). **Human Error**; Cambridge University Press New York, USA

Schein, E.H. (2003). **Organisationskultur**; The Ed Schein Corporate Culture Survival Guide; MIT/Cambridge USA; Edition Humanistische Psychologie, Bergisch Gladbach

Seghezzi, H. D. (1996). **Integriertes Qualitätsmanagement**; Das St. Galler Konzept München; Hanser Verlag München

Seghezzi, H.D. (2008). **Integriertes Qualitätsmanagement**; Der St. Galler Ansatz; 3. völlig überarbeitete Auflage; Hanser Verlag München

Senge, P. (2008). **Die fünfte Disziplin**; Die Kunst und Praxis der Lernenden Organisation; Schöffer-Poeschel, 10. Auflage

Strunz, H. / Dorsch, M. (2001). **Management**; Managementwissen für Studium und Praxis, Oldenburg Wissenschaftsverlag München

Vester, F. (2007). **Die Kunst vernetzt zu denken**; Ideen und Werkzeuge für einen neuen Umgang mit Komplexität, 6. Auflage, dtv Verlag, München

Wallmüller, E. (2001). **Software Qualitätsmanagement in der Praxis**; 2., völlig überarbeitete Auflage, Hanser Verlag München

Wallmüller, E. (2011). **Software Quality Engineering**; ein Leitfaden für bessere Software Qualität; 3. Auflage Hanser Verlag München